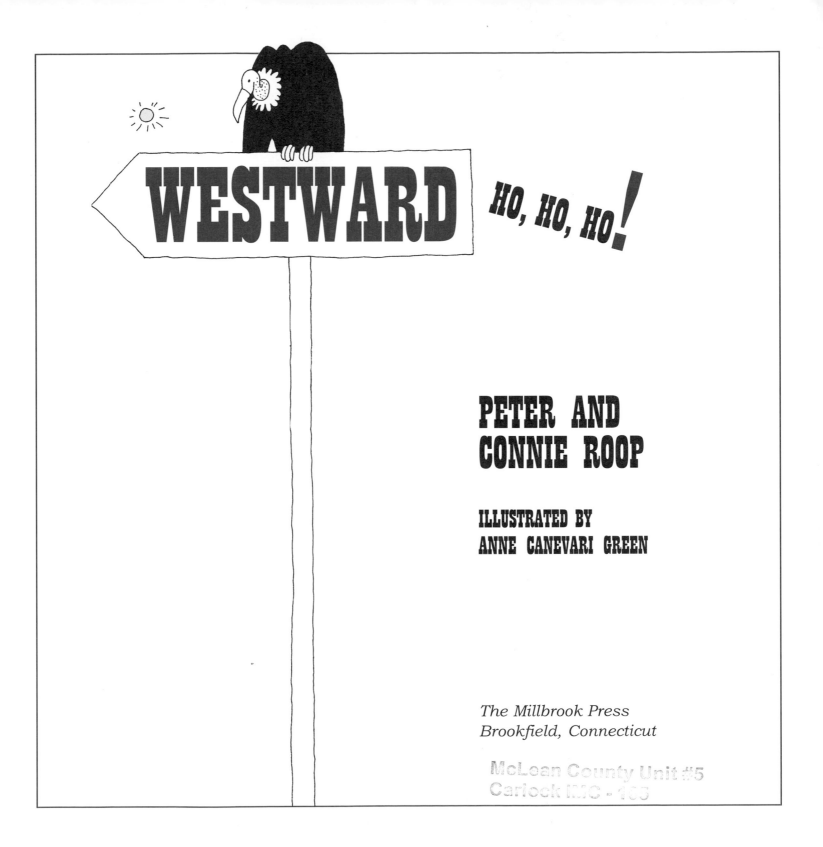

WESTWARD

HO, HO, HO!

PETER AND
CONNIE ROOP

ILLUSTRATED BY
ANNE CANEVARI GREEN

The Millbrook Press
Brookfield, Connecticut

For Father, a cowboy at heart.
Giddyup, Danny!

Library of Congress Cataloging-in-Publication Data
Roop, Peter.
Westward, ho, ho, ho! / by Peter and Connie Roop; illustrated by Anne
Canevari Green.
    p. cm.
    Summary: presents essays, jokes, riddles, and suggested readings on
aspects of the Wild West, from the Oregon Trail to the Alamo, from Native
Americans to cowboys, from explorers to outlaws.
    ISBN 0-7613-0020-1 (lib. bdg.)
    1. West (U.S.) — History—To 1848—Juvenile literature. 2. West (U.S.)—
History—1848–1950—Juvenile literature. 3. Frontier and pioneer life—
West (U.S.)—Juvenile literature. 4. West (U.S.)—History—To 1848—
Juvenile humor. 5. West (U.S.) History—1848–1950—Juvenile humor. 6.
Frontier and pioneer life—West (U.S.)—Juvenile humor. [1. West (U.S.)—
History. 2. Frontier and pioneer life—West (U.S.) 3. West (U.S.)—History—
Wit and humor. 4. Frontier and pioneer life—West (U.S.)—Wit and humor.
5. Jokes. 6. Riddles.] I. Roop, Connie. II. Green, Anne Canevari, ill. III.
Title.
F592.R66   1996   978—dc20   95-48315   CIP   AC

Published by The Millbrook Press, Inc.
2 Old New Milford Road, Brookfield, Connecticut 06804
Copyright ©1996 by Peter and Connie Roop
Illustrations copyright © 1996 by Anne Canevari Green

CONTENTS

INTRODUCTION

Take a journey through the Wild West and have fun along the way! From Oregon to the Alamo, from Native Americans to cowboys, from explorers to outlaws, you will meet the people and visit the places that made the West such a wild place.

Each of these fifteen mini-reports briefly highlights one aspect of the West. You can follow in the footsteps of Lewis and Clark or share the hardships of pioneer women. You can thrill to the sharpshooting of Annie Oakley or rush to find gold. You can remember the Alamo or glimpse Native American life.

These brief reports are written to whet your appetite to explore the West on your own. Each essay ends with a bibliography of other books and magazines you can use to track down more information about the West.

And you'll have fun along the trail! Like nuggets from the gold rush, Wild West jokes are scattered along the way. These jokes are certain to hit the bull's eye of your sense of humor. But beware! Some of them just might be fool's gold!

Have a safe journey through the Wild West. And remember what Santa Claus said as he headed for the Sante Fe Trail: "Westward ho, ho, ho!"

I FOUND IT AND I NAMED IT, BUT I'LL BE DURNED IF I'M GOING TO CLIMB THE DING-DANGED THING...

PIKE'S PEAK

ZEB

A gentle breeze pushes the three boats up the wide Missouri River. Aboard are Meriwether Lewis, William Clark, and about thirty hardy young men, including Clark's slave, York. Lewis carries orders from President Thomas Jefferson to explore the Louisiana Territory, which the United States has just purchased from France. He also has instructions to find a way across America from the Mississippi River to the Pacific Ocean.

On May 14, 1804, the adventure begins. Two years and 8,000 miles (12,900 kilometers) later, Lewis and Clark and all but one of the men return safely. Heroes now, they reached the Pacific and returned to share their knowledge and adventures.

Hundreds of mountain men, traders, and explorers went west next. They wandered the West in search of furs or easy routes to the Pacific. They became the first white men to see the West's spectacular natural beauties. Fur trapper John Colter warmed himself at Yellowstone's hot springs. Zebulon Pike named a 14,110-foot (4,300-meter) mountain after himself (he never climbed Pike's Peak). Mountain man Joe Walker, the first white man to gaze on the wonders of Yosemite, remembered that moment as the best of his adventuresome life. These men did not follow trails but made them.

John Fremont, who became widely known as the "Pathfinder," was one of many trailblazers looking for a route to the Pacific. He blazed one of the first trails to Oregon and California. Pike, after naming his peak, made tracks to Santa Fe, beginning the Sante Fe Trail.

Not all western explorers were as fortunate as Lewis and Clark. Some went west never to be heard from again—lost in a desert, injured, killed by an arrow. Others, finding lush green meadows, gave up wandering and settled down to farm.

No matter their reasons, these men opened the West for millions of pioneers, miners, and settlers to follow in their footsteps.

JOKES

What has four eyes but still can't see?
The Mississippi.

How did Pike first see the mountains?
He peeked.

Trapper: That is a baby snake over yonder.
Trader: How can you tell?
Trapper: By its rattles!

What is a snake's favorite subject in school?
Hiss-tory.

How did Lewis know the big cat wasn't telling the truth?
It was a mountain lyin'.

Lewis: How can you keep a skunk from smelling?
Clark: Cut off its nose!

Lewis: What can run but never walk?
Clark: The Missouri River.

What did Santa say to Lewis and Clark?
"Westward ho, ho, ho!"

Why did William Clark have such good weather during his trip?
Because he took along "Merry Weather" Lewis!

Blumberg, Rhoda. *Incredible Journey of Lewis and Clark.* Lothrop, 1991.
Roop, Peter, and Connie Roop. *Off the Map: The Journals of Lewis and Clark.* Walker, 1993.
Seymour, Flora. *Sacagawea: American Pathfinder.* Simon and Schuster, 1991.

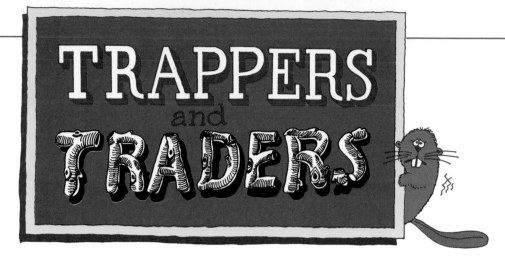

TRAPPERS and TRADERS

All at once the aspen tree falls. Splash! A beaver wades into the water and gnaws off branches. One by one it pulls them underwater and sticks their pointed ends into the mud. These branches will help feed its family over the long winter months. Going back for more, the beaver does not see or smell the steel trap. It clamps down on a front paw. The doomed beaver tries to free itself. Before it can gnaw off its own foot, the beaver drowns.

The next morning a trapper, dressed in buckskins, finds the beaver. He feels its thick fur pelt. "Make a nice hat for some fancy man in London," he says to himself as he skins the beaver with his sharp knife. "Worth four dollars at least."

The skins of beaver, deer, fox, mink, lynx, otter, and other animal furs were treasured by Europeans. The trade in valuable furs lured explorers farther and farther into the American wilderness. Native Americans, expert trappers themselves, traded furs for blankets, iron kettles, guns, bullets, steel traps, and other goods.

French, British, and American trappers were the first white men to wander through the West. Eager to find new sources of furs, especially beaver, they followed rivers and streams into the heart of the wilderness.

Traders followed in the footsteps of the trappers. These men—in canoes, on foot, or on horseback—traded with Native Americans and white trappers. Once their trade goods were gone, they returned to more settled areas to sell the furs. Shiploads of western furs then crossed the Atlantic to be made into hats, leather goods, and expensive capes by eager Europeans.

Silk hats put the fur trappers out of business in the mid-nineteenth century. Soon after, the hardy trappers disappeared, their way of life over. With the arrival of the pioneers the traders stayed in business, supplying the settlers with everything from needles to plows.

JOKES

What has many sharp teeth but no mouth?
A saw.

Trapper: What should you do if a grizzly bear charges you?
Hunter: Pay him!

What side of a buffalo has the most fur?
The outside!

Trader: If you were walking in the forest and a grizzly bear came after you, would you walk back to town or run?
Trapper: I'd sure run.
Trader: With a bear behind?

If a trapper was born In France, grew up in Canada, moved to the United States, and died in Montana, what is he?
Dead.

Hunter: I met the biggest grizzly in the forest today!
Trapper: Did you give him both barrels?
Hunter: Both barrels? No way, I gave him the whole gun.

What did the trapper look like after he shaved?
Bear.

Why did the trader ride his horse across the desert?
Because he couldn't carry it!

Mother Grizzly: Son, what are you doing?
Young Grizzly: Chasing a hunter around a tree.
Mother Grizzly: How many times do I have to tell you not to play with your food?

"Mountain Men." *Cobblestone* Magazine. December, 1991.
Editors, Time-Life Books. *Frontiersmen.* Time-Life Books, 1977.
Stewart, Gail. *Trappers and Traders.* Rourke, 1990.
Stewart, Gail. *Frontiersmen.* Rourke, 1990.

NATIVE AMERICANS

Cornflower, a Navajo, steps out of her hogan door. The red rock walls of the canyon tower above her. It is early, and long shadows still fill the canyon. Picking up her staff, she lets the sheep out of the corral and herds them along the stream. She will take the sheep up the canyon to graze on fresh grass. Cornflower greets her mother as she waters the family's maize (corn), beans, and watermelons. Maybe tonight her father and brothers will return from herding horses on the mesa. Maybe Grandfather will tell about his time among the strange people who live far to the north, people who live in homes that move. She smiles as she says, "Tepee."

From Canada to Mexico, from the Mississippi to the Pacific lived dozens of different Native American tribes. The land, weather, and animals greatly influenced how these Native Americans lived.

On the northern and central plains, the Blackfeet, Crow, Cheyenne, Sioux, Omaha, Comanche, and other, smaller tribes followed the great herds of migrating buffalo. The Mandan built permanent homes and grew crops along the Missouri. In the desert southwest the Navajo, Apache, Zuni, and Hopi built hogans or pueblos; raised horses, sheep, and goats; and grew crops. In the wet northwest the Chinook built great homes of cedar. Salmon, deer, and elk provided them with food. In sunny California acorns, birds, elk, deer, and fish fed the Pomo who lived in grass and wood huts.

The western Native Americans spoke many different languages. By means of silent signs the different tribes of the Plains could talk with one another.

Unfortunately for the Native Americans, white settlers wanted their lands. Treaty after treaty was made between the Native Americans and the United States, only to be broken when gold or silver was discovered on Native American land or settlers wanted the land for farms. In 1845 Native Americans lived free in the West. By 1900, through warfare and starvation, the surviving Native Americans, once proud masters of the West, had been forced onto reservations.

JOKES

What is the best month to plant Native American corn?
May is (maize).

How did the Native Americans make fifteen baskets of corn from one basket?
They popped it.

What could speak every Native American language?
An echo.

What two letters name a Sioux home?
T P.

How did the Native Americans know when buffalo were coming?
They herd them.

Trapper: Can we cross the Missouri?
Native American: I can. Canoe?

What part of a salmon weighs the most?
The scales.

Where did the Native Americans go for ice cream?
Custard's Last Stand.

What goes through the forest without making a sound?
A path.

What is as big as a tepee but lighter than an eagle's feather?
The tepee's shadow!

Freedman, Russell. *Indian Chiefs*. Holiday House, 1988.
Hoyt-Goldsmith, Diane. *Pueblo Storyteller*. Holiday House, 1991.
McGovern, Ann. *If You Lived With the Sioux.....* Four Winds, 1972.
Wolfson, Evelyn. *The Teton Sioux*. Millbrook Press, 1992.

BUFFALO

Small Deer pinches his knees against his horse's flanks. His left hand holds his bows, his right the reins. He glances at the buffalo herd grazing on the grass below the ridge. Small Deer looks back at the hunt leader, whose hand is raised.

Suddenly the hand drops. Small Deer kicks his horse. It leaps forward. All around him the other hunters join the chase. The buffalo hunt is on. Small Deer hopes today he will make his first kill.

The buffalo was a store on hooves for the Plains Native Americans. A successful hunt provided the people with fresh meat, hides for clothing and tepees, horns for spoons and decorations, and bones for tools. For the Blackfeet, Sioux, Cheyenne, Crow, Mandan, and other Plains tribes the sacred buffalo meant life.

Before the Spanish brought horses to North America, the Native Americans hunted buffalo on foot or by driving a herd over a cliff. Only a few animals at a time could be killed this way. Tribes had to be constantly on the move, following the herds in the hopes of killing some. However, on horseback, the hunters could charge into a herd and bring down many more buffalo than they could on foot. With food more available, the lives of the Plains Native Americans became easier.

The coming of the white people ended the glory days of the Plains Native Americans. White hunters slaughtered the buffalo by the millions for meat, hides, tongues, or just sport. Once huge herds roamed, herds so large it took days for all to pass. But by 1883 buffalo were scarce. Many Native Americans, facing starvation now that their food supply was cut off, reluctantly went onto reservations.

By 1900, fewer than 1,000 buffalo remained. The efforts of several ranchers saved those so that today from Wisconsin to California, small private herds range where mighty herds once thundered.

JOKES

How did the hunters pay for buffalo?
With buffalo bills.

What is buffalo hide used for?
To hold the buffalo together.

How do you get down from a buffalo?
You can't get down from a buffalo. You get down from a goose.

What does a buffalo calf become after it is one year old?
Two years old!

Why did the hunter buy a map of New York state?
He was looking for Buffalo.

How did the pioneer stop the angry buffalo from charging?
She took away his charge card.

Why can't a buffalo dance?
It has two left feet.

What was the buffalo doing on the highway last night?
About ten miles an hour.

"The Story of America's Buffalo." *Cobblestone* Magazine. August, 1981.
Freedman, Russell. *Buffalo Hunt*. Holiday House, 1988.
Patent, Dorothy Hinshaw. *Buffalo: The American Bison*. Clarion, 1986.

THE OREGON TRAIL

"**W**estward ho!" shouts the wagon master.

"Oregon or Bust!" cheer the pioneers. Fathers fire their rifles into the air. Mothers herd young children onto the wagons. Boys and girls race ahead on the trail. One by one the heavily loaded wagons begin rolling down the Oregon Trail.

Five months later, across 2,000 miles (3,200 kilometers) of prairie, mountains, plains, and desert, the surviving settlers reach Oregon, the end of the trail.

The Oregon Trail stretched from Independence, Missouri, to the Oregon frontier. From 1840, thousands of pioneers, trappers, traders, and adventurers traveled the trail. Along the way, over 34,000 people died, 17 for every mile (nearly 11 people for every kilometer) of the tortuous trail.

Why did these folks follow the Oregon Trail? For many, Oregon meant fine farmland and a chance to make a better life for themselves and their families. For others, the trail meant danger and adventure. Some went to escape a life of poverty, others went to get rich. No matter the reason, reaching the end of the Oregon Trail alive meant the beginning of a new life.

JOKES

What train had no tracks?
A wagon train.

What did the canvas say to the wagon?
"Don't move. I've got you covered."

Why were the poor settlers stuck on one side of the Missouri River?
They couldn't a-ford to cross.

Why did the pioneer put an egg on the neck of his ox?
He needed a new yoke.

Why did the pioneer burn his broken rifle?
So it would fire.

What did the butcher say to the pioneer's pig?
"Go West, young ham!"

Why did thc pioneers let their cattle drive their wagons?
Because they could steer.

What kind of ice cream did the pioneers eat along the Oregon Trail?
Rocky Road.

Pioneer: Do we stop when we reach the Missouri River?
Wagon master: If we don't, there will be one heck of a splash!

Three pioneers fell out of the wagon when crossing the Platte River. Only two got their hair wet. Why?
One of the pioneers was bald.

When is a pioneer's dog like his cart?
When his tail is a waggin'.

"The Oregon Trail." *Cobblestone* Magazine. December, 1991.
Fisher, Leonard Everett. *The Oregon Trail*. Holiday House, 1990.
Stein, Conrad. *The Oregon Trail*. Childrens Press, 1984.

THE CALIFORNIA GOLD RUSH

James Marshall works at Mr. Sutter's mill in California. Suddenly he puts down his hammer. He glimpses a stone glittering below. He picks up the dime-sized stone and turns it over in his hand. The yellow rock feels unusually heavy. Is it gold?

Yes!

Marshall's discovery of gold sent thousands of fortune hunters flooding into California to try their luck. "There's gold in them thar hills!" and "California or Bust!" cried shopkeepers, farmers, clerks, husbands, wives, soldiers, sailors, and candlestick makers as they rushed to California in 1849. The Forty-niners were on their way! The gold rush was on.

Armed with shovels, picks, axes, knives, even spoons, the Forty-niners staked their claims and grubbed in the ground for the elusive gold. A miner could stake a claim to no more than 50 square feet (15 square meters) of land.

The first miners got the easy gold, the gold lying in the streambeds. Some found pieces of gold the size of peas, or nuggets as large as eggs. Most found flakes of gold. The largest solid piece discovered weighed 194 pounds (87 kilograms)! When the easy pickings were gone, the rocks and sand were panned. Miners stood in the near-freezing water swirling pans of sand, hoping to catch the glitter of a flake or two. Some miners dammed streams to search the dry beds. Others dug great holes.

Mining towns grew like mushrooms after a rain. Angels Camp, Murder's Bar, Poverty Hill, Fiddletown, Whiskey Flat, Nevada City sprouted where rich strikes were discovered.

Life in the mining towns was hard. Prices were high. One Forty-niner paid over eleven dollars for two potatoes and a jar of pickles. A box of sardines cost sixteen dollars. Hotels were crowded, the men sleeping three to a bed.

Many people got wealthy not from mining, but from selling supplies and meals to miners. Levi Strauss arrived in California with blue canvas for tents.

Realizing that his canvas would make good, strong pants for the miners, Strauss made the first blue jeans and a fortune.

Between 1848 and 1852, more than $250,000,000 in gold was dug up. However, only a few Forty-niners struck it rich. Many miners returned home poorer than when they left. Many, however, made enough money to settle in California, often sending for their families back East to join them. By 1850 so many people had moved to California that it became a state.

JOKES

Why did the miner call a doctor?
He had gold fever.

What is a miner's favorite football team?
The 49ers.

Why did so many people hurry to California?
They were in a rush.

Why did the miner quit playing baseball?
He struck out.

How are miners and dentists alike?
They both like to drill.

How much gold could a miner put in an empty sack?
A nugget. After that the sack won't be empty.

What is a miner's favorite fish?
Goldfish.

Why do miners like fall?
That's when the leaves turn to gold.

What did the hippie miner say after he staked a claim?
I can dig it!

"California History." *Cobblestone* Magazine. May, 1985.
Blumberg, Rhoda. *The Great American Gold Rush.* Bradbury, 1989.
Stein, Conrad. *The California Gold Rush.* Childrens Press, 1995.

THE SOLDIERS

"Yiiiii!"

The fierce war cry cuts across the camp. The U.S. Army soldiers, barely awake, grab their repeating rifles and begin firing at the charging Sioux. Horses neigh as bullets smack into the ground and rip through tents. Here and there a soldier falls, dead or wounded.

"Pull back to the island," orders the lieutenant. His small force of thirty-five men splashes across the stream, pulling their horses with them. Digging into the sand with plates, the soldiers mound up dirt. They watch and wait as the Native Americans regroup and prepare to charge.

Once again the air filled with war cries, the crackle of gunfire, the moaning of the wounded, and the frightened whinnies of the horses.

Scenes like this happened over and over in the West. Ordered by the United States to subdue the Native Americans, the soldiers fought the native people in battles, small and large. Equally determined not to give up their homelands, the Native Americans naturally resisted.

Life was not easy for the soldiers. There were vast distances to cover, either on foot or horseback. The food was terrible. Hard biscuits, beans, fresh meat if the hunters were lucky. There were raging storms and baking heat to suffer. There was the loneliness of being far from home. The pay was poor, only thirteen dollars a month. And there was always the danger of battle.

Yet still they came. Bookkeepers, farm boys, store clerks, blacksmiths, immigrants, and freed slaves joined up. Black soldiers formed four regiments. The Native Americans called the black troopers "Buffalo Soldiers." This was because they respected the blacks so much for their fighting ability that they linked the soldiers to their sacred buffalo, and because the Buffalo Soldiers' hair reminded them of the buffalo's fur.

Eager for adventure, needing a job, or running from something, thousands of men and boys went west as soldiers.

JOKES

Why did the soldier put a saddle on a bear?
He wanted to ride bearback.

Tom: That snake bit me!
John: Did you put anything on it?
Tom: No, he liked me the way I was!

Captain: Name me an old-time settler in the West.
Private: The sun.

What was the fastest way for a soldier to double his dollars?
Fold them!

What did Mrs. Bullet say to Mr. Bullet?
"Honey, we are going to have a BB."

Why was Nate Rogers Grant never tired?
Because his initials give him NRG!

What did the rifle say to the pistol?
"My pop is bigger than your pop!"

What was the most dangerous season for the cavalry?
Fall.

If one soldier had a whole apple, and another soldier had only a bite, what should he do?
Scratch it!

Why did the young soldier's mother knit him three socks?
He wrote and told her he had grown another foot.

"Buffalo Soldiers." Cobblestone Magazine. February, 1995.
Editors, Time-Life Books. *Soldiers.* Time-Life Books, 1973.

Cowboys

"**G**it along little dogie!" a cowboy shouts at a calf. "Cookie will have the chuck wagon cleaned up before we reach camp." He yanks on the lariat around the calf's neck and touches his spurs to his horse's flanks. The calf bellows as it follows the horse and rider into the sunset. Another day's work is done for the cowboy.

Between the years 1865 and 1885, over 40,000 cowboys rounded cattle, drove cattle, and cared for cattle in the Old West. Who were these hardworking men who braved stampedes, suffered scorching summer days, and endured freezing blizzards? Some were Civil War soldiers, both Yankees and Rebels. Some were Mexicans carrying on their traditional jobs. One out of every six cowboys was black; many freed slaves at the end of the Civil War found a new life herding cattle on the Great Plains.

A cowboy's life revolved around the seasons. In spring he would roam the range tracking down the ranch's horses. During the winter most of the horses ran free. In spring they had to be rounded up and corraled. The cowboys knew which horses were theirs by the animals' brands. Each horse had the special mark of its ranch burned into its hide.

Once the horses were ready, the cowboys rounded up the cattle and newly born calves. With shouts and twirling lariats, they rounded up every cow and steer bearing the ranch's brand.

Newly born calves then had to be branded. One cowboy roped the calf, another held it down, and a third touched the calf's side with a hot branding iron. Now the calf was marked with its owner's brand.

In the fall, the cattle, fat on summer grass, had to be rounded up and driven to market. The cowboys followed special trails on these drives. Over half of the cattle from Texas moved along the famous Chisholm Trail, which stretched hundreds of miles from Brownsville, Texas, to Abilene, Kansas.

Even in the winter the cattle still had to be cared for. Hay and salt were carried to them. Some animals had to be dug out of snowdrifts. Then when spring came again the whole cycle repeated itself.

Being a cowboy in the Old West was hard work. But there were also lazy moments in the bunkhouse, stomach-stuffing meals at the chuck wagon, tall tales told at the campfire, and the wide open spaces of the Wild West to enjoy.

JOKES

Name a famous cowboy cook.
Chuck Wagon.

Why did the cowboy buy a dachshund at the rodeo?
He wanted to git a long little dogie.

Why did the cowboy put bells on his cows?
Because the horns didn't work.

What part of a steer is invisible?
Its hide.

What is a cowboy's favorite car?
A Mustang.

How does a cowboy take a wrinkle out of a cow?
With a branding iron.

What is a cowboy's favorite salad dressing?
Ranch.

What did the cowboy's guitar say to him?
"Why are you always picking on me?"

Big Cow: I just can't get over what I saw last night.
Little Cow: What did you see?
Big Cow: The moon.

"Cowboys." *Cobblestone* Magazine. July, 1982.

Freedman, Russell. *Cowboys of the Wild West.* Houghton Mifflin, 1985.

Marrin, Albert. *Cowboys, Indians, and Gunfighters: The Story of the Cattle Kingdom.* Simon and Schuster, 1992.

Miller, Robert. *Reflections of a Black Cowboy.* Silver Burdett, 1992.

TRAILS WEST

"Head 'em up. Move 'em out," yells the trail boss. The cowboys spur their horses on, shouting and smacking their hats. Slowly the herd of cattle begins moving north. The cattle moo, the dust rises, and the cowboys ride. Another trail drive begins.

The dusty, rutted, winding trails of the West were like today's highways. They crossed the open plains and steep mountain passes. Trappers, traders, explorers, Native Americans, pioneers, miners, armies, and cattle walked or rode along these trails.

The Chisholm, Santa Fe, Oregon, El Camino Real, Bozeman, and Mormon trails are the best known. Each trail had its own highs and lows. Some, like the Camino Real in California, connected settlements in one region. Others, like the Chisholm, were for driving cattle from their grazing ranges to market. The Mormon Trail led the Mormons and others to Utah. The Bozeman, Santa Fe, and Oregon trails led pioneers and miners west to find new homes or strike it rich.

Many of the trails were littered with household goods too heavy to carry any farther in covered wagons. Bleached bones of dead oxen and cattle lined some trails. Dirt or rock mounds marked the graves of travelers who died on the way.

The trails were dangerous. Blinding duststorms or freezing blizzards caught many travelers. Native Americans, determined to keep the whites out of their lands, attacked. Stampeding buffalo or cattle presented other hazards. No matter the danger, wagons rolled and cattle moved on the trails. Each trail was unique, but they all served as western highways.

JOKES

Why did the wagon keep doing the same thing over and over again?
It was in a rut.

What has two heads, one tail, six feet, and four ears?
A trailblazer on a horse.

What two letters describe the desert?
M T.

Why did the pioneer's rooster refuse to fight?
It was chicken!

Why is a wild horse like an egg?
They must both be broken before they can be used.

Will: Does your horse have fleas?
Bill: Don't be silly. Horses don't have fleas—they have colts.

Why did the cowboy take a hammer to bed with him?
So he could hit the hay.

Why could the Rocky Mountains hear so well?
Because it had mountaineers.

Will: That shiny star is Mars.
Bill: The other one must be Pa's.

"The Sante Fe Trail." *Cobblestone* Magazine. May, 1990.
Editors, Time-Life Books. *Trails West.* Time-Life Books, 1977.
Levine, Ellen. *If You Traveled West in a Covered Wagon....* Scholastic, 1992.

Women of the Wild West

The sun rises over the prairie. A pioneer woman picks up a dried buffalo chip and puts it in her wheelbarrow. At her sod home she feeds the chickens, gets a bucket of water from the creek, puts four buffalo chips on the fire, and cooks breakfast. She finally wakes her eight children and husband. Her day has just begun.

Thousands of western women, white and black, began their days much like this. Most came with their husbands to settle the plains and raise their families. Their days were filled with backbreaking chores: cooking, washing, cleaning, planting crops, drawing water, milking cows, making clothes, caring for the sick or injured. The chores never ended.

Not every woman who came west, however, was a pioneer. Many young women went west to teach and maybe find a husband. Others roped cattle, hunted buffalo, panned for gold, ran restaurants, did laundry for miners, danced in saloons, or even robbed banks.

One of the most famous western women was Calamity Jane. She refused to wear women's clothes, preferring the freedom of men's pants and shirts. Armed with a pistol and rifle, Jane roped cattle, drove a mail coach, and scouted for the army. For a time she even worked in a Wild West show.

Life was not any easier for Native American women. Their days, too, were full of endless tasks. They planted corn, beans, and squash. They cut up buffalo meat, cooked it, preserved it, and dried the skins. They made their families' clothes and tepees from the buffalo hides. They gathered berries and dug roots. When it was time to move, they took down the tepees and loaded the horses. When a new camping area was found, the women set up the tepees and organized the home.

Whether white, black, or native, women were essential to the successful settlement of the West.

What did the pioneer say when she saw the cupboard was empty?
"O-I-C-U-R-M-T."

Why did the pioneer woman put her chickens in a coop?
They were using fowl language!

What did the Native American girl lose every time she stood up?
Her lap.

Why did the pioneer woman name her rooster Robinson?
Because he Crusoe.

Teacher: Students, someone please give a sentence with lovable in it.
Pioneer Boy: If anyone knows how to love a bull, please tell me.

What did the porcupine say to the cactus?
"Is that you, Mama?"

What did the pioneer woman grow in the garden when she worked hard?
Tired.

Why didn't pioneer women become bald as soon as pioneer men?
They wore their hair longer.

Teacher: Johnny, name four things that contain milk.
Johnny: Cheese, milk, and…two cows!

What did pioneer women call little black cats?
Kittens!

How was the pioneer cruel to her corn?
She pulled its ears.

Freedman, Russell. *Children of the Wild West*. Clarion, 1983.
Harvey, Brett. *My Prairie Year*. Scholastic, 1993.
Savage, Jeff. *Pioneering Women of the Wild West*. Enslow, 1995.

THE PONY EXPRESS

The cloud of dust, a black speck in its center, grows larger. The two men holding the reins of a swift pony can just make out the Pony Express rider. Minutes later, the sweating horse and dusty rider thunder up. The slim rider snatches the mail pouches off his horse, slings them onto the fresh pony, mounts, and gallops off. The two men watch the new dust cloud disappear in the distance. Another Pony Express relay is finished.

The Pony Express, the most famous mail route in American history, crossed 1,800 miles (2,880 kilometers) of plains, deserts, and mountains between St. Joseph, Missouri, in the East and Sacramento, California, in the West. For one dollar, a half-ounce (24-gram) letter could make the distance in ten days. This beat the twenty-five days the same letter would take if carried by stagecoach. Letters were written on very thin paper. Newspapers, too, had to be printed on special lightweight paper. The letters were carried in locked, leather pouches that were unopened from the beginning to the end of the ride. It took forty riders heading east and forty riders heading west to keep the Pony Express on time.

The 500 horses ridden were fast. They carried the lightweight riders 5 to 10 miles (8 to 16 kilometers) between stations. The riders were adventuresome young men, all under eighteen years old and slim. Not an extra ounce could be carried on the Pony Express. Fifteen-year-old Buffalo Bill was one of the most famous riders. One day, after being stopped by bandits, he tricked them into chasing him and raced 324 miles (522 kilometers).

Chased by Native Americans and held up by robbers, the Pony Express riders had to be brave. Through storms, over burning deserts, and across flooded streams, the mail had to go through. And it did.

But it wasn't the dangers, land, or weather that ended the Pony Express. The dots and dashes of the telegraph could carry messages much faster than horses. So in 1861, when the first telegraph wires stretched from east to west, the Pony Express ended. After operating for only eighteen months, the Pony Express rode into the sunset of American history.

JOKES

What do we call stories about horses?
Pony tales.

Clem: I forgot my gloves!
Lem: Why didn't you tie a string around your finger?
Clem: Gloves are warmer!

What did Buffalo Bill say after his 324-mile ride?
"Whoa!"

Why were Pony Express riders so funny?
They were always horsing around.

Why did the new Pony Express rider put wings on his horse?
He wanted to see a horsefly.

Who always goes to sleep with his shoes on?
A horse.

What is the most important part of a horse?
The mane part.

Dan: Did you hear about the stagecoach without any wheels?
Sam: What held it up?
Dan: Outlaws.

If a Pony Express rider saw twenty Native Americans chasing a buffalo across the prairie, what time was it?
Twenty after one!

Little Boy: Do you have a letter for me?
Pony Express Rider: What is your name?
Little Boy: It will be on the letter.

First Rider: I fell off while I was riding!
Second Rider: Horseback?
First Rider: I don't know. I'll see when I get back to the stable.

"The Pony Express" *Cobblestone* Magazine. October, 1981.
Savage, Jeff. *Pony Express Riders of the Wild West.* Enslow, 1995.
Stein, Conrad. *The Pony Express.* Childrens Press, 1976.

I'VE BEEN WORKIN' ON THE RAILROAD

On May 10, 1869, two steaming train engines face each other at Promontory Point, Utah. Between them a man swings his sledgehammer, driving in a golden spike. This special spike is the last of millions of iron spikes holding down the steel rails that finally crossed America. Stretching from Omaha, Nebraska, to Sacramento, California, this railroad opened the West for settlers, miners, cattlemen, businessmen, and sightseeing travelers.

Laying the wooden ties and steel rails for the "Iron Horse" cost millions of dollars and took millions of acres of land, but it united the East and the West.

"I've been workin' on the railroad" could have been sung by the thousands of Civil War veterans, freed slaves, Native Americans, Chinese, and European immigrants who built the railroads. Up, over, even through mountains, across burning deserts, over wide rivers the railroad men slowly laid the tracks. Four rails a minute, 100 spikes, 400 rails a mile (62 spikes, 248 rails a kilometer). For thirty-five dollars a month per man, a good crew could lay more than 2 miles (3.25 kilometers) a day, depending on how flat the land was. The record of 643 miles (1,035 kilometers) in less than eight months still stands.

Much happened before a rail was spiked. First, a survey crew planned out the best route. Then, armed with shovels, picks, and dynamite, another crew dug earth, blasted tunnels, and bridged rivers. Finally, the rails were laid and spiked down.

At long last, that May day, when the golden spike was driven, the first of five transcontinental railroads was finished. By 1890, more than 70,000 miles (112,700 kilometers) of railroad track went west from the Mississippi River to the Pacific Ocean.

JOKES

What did the railroad man find in the middle of America?
The letter R.

What went all the way from Kansas to California without moving an inch?
The railroad tracks.

Why is baseball like the cook's biscuit?
It depends on the batter.

Why did the two train tracks never meet?
Nobody introduced them.

Passenger: Is this my train?
Conductor: No, Sir. It belongs to the Central Pacific Company.

Passenger: Can I take this train to Sacramento?
Conductor: No, Ma'am. It's much too heavy.

Engineer: I'm so dirty. Where can I bathe?
Conductor: In the spring.
Engineer: I didn't ask you when. I asked you where!

Why can trains hear so well?
They have engineers.

What did the engine say to the coal car?
"Let's get hitched!"

Why did the dynamiter like his job so much?
It was a blast.

What do steam engines eat?
Coal cuts.

What did the mother engine say to her child?
"Don't forget to choo, choo your food!"

"Transcontinental Railroad." *Cobblestone* Magazine. May, 1980.

Fisher, Leonard Everett. *Tracks Across America: The Story of the American Railroad.* Holiday House, 1989.

Gintzler, A. S. *Rough and Ready Railroaders.* John Muir, 1995.

ANNIE OAKLEY

Annie Oakley, in a fringed skirt and cowboy hat, raises her rifle. Her husband throws five glass balls into the air. Bang! Bang! Bang! Bang! Bang! Each ball shatters. Her husband holds up a dime. Bang! A hole right through the center. Using a knife blade as a mirror, Annie looks backward over her shoulder. Bang! The glass ball in her husband's hand blows apart. For her last shot, her husband puts a cigarette in his mouth. Bang! The cigarette disappears.

Little Sure Shot, as Chief Sitting Bull called Annie Oakley, once again proves she is the best shot in the West.

Born Annie Moses in 1860, Annie changed her name when she became a professional sharpshooter. The name Oakley came from the Cincinnati suburb where Annie once lived. Annie had not planned to be a sharpshooter when she grew up. After her father died, her poor family had little food on the table. Determined to help, Annie first trapped rabbits. Then one day, with her brother's help, she loaded and fired her father's heavy rifle. The roast squirrel that night was delicious! After much practice—and many dead turkeys, pheasants, partridges, and squirrels—Annie Oakley traveled around the country, showing off her remarkable shooting skills.

BUFFALO BILL

Thirteen-year-old Bill Cody chases a runaway horse. Bringing it back to the wagon train, he sees a buffalo charging the camp. He raises his rifle and pulls the trigger. The buffalo crashes to the ground. Buffalo Bill Cody has shot his first buffalo.

At fifteen, this adventuresome teen carried the mail from Missouri to California as a Pony Express rider. He enjoyed the danger of racing storms, outriding Native Americans, and galloping fast. By twenty-two, Cody was a scout for the army. Then he turned his talents to hunting buffalo for the hungry men building railroads across the wide West. In eight months Bill shot 4,280 buffalo. He was now Buffalo Bill.

But even this was not enough action for Bill. Always a showman, he put together a thrilling show with real cowboys, Native Americans (including his old enemy Sitting Bull), horses, buffalo, sharpshooters, and stagecoaches. Buffalo Bill's Wild West Show toured America and Europe, performing for presidents, kings, and queens. For over thirty years this remarkable hunter, rider, sharpshooter, and showman entertained tens of thousands of people, all of whom wanted a safe glimpse of the Wild West.

SITTING BULL

Sitting Bull, Dakota Sioux holy man and chief, sits outside his tepee. Hundreds of other tepees stretch along the Little Bighorn River. His people know that the U.S. Army Cavalry is nearby. The Native Americans will not fight unless first attacked. Sitting Bull has a vision, a vision of white men falling into the Sioux camp. His vision means Native American victory.

Under the leadership of Sitting Bull (he did not fight) and Crazy Horse (he fought), the Native Americans defeat General George Custer when he attacks, wiping out all 220 men under his command. Sitting Bull's vision was true.

Sitting Bull had long been a Sioux leader. When he was fourteen, he counted his first coup by touching an enemy during a battle and escaping unharmed. Courageous, wise, and caring, Sitting Bull was respected more than any other Sioux chief. A brave warrior, Sitting Bull was also an important medicine man, a holy person who worked to better the lives of his people.

Early in his life Sitting Bull had not wanted war with the white people. He hoped they would leave the Sioux in peace to follow the old ways and hunt buffalo. But when the United States tried to make the Sioux give up their way of life, Sitting Bull led those who refused "to walk the white man's way." He smoked the warpipe with Red Cloud, Crazy Horse, and Roman Nose, all promising to fight the whites to their deaths.

After the Sioux defeated Custer, the U.S. Army came after Sitting Bull. Sitting Bull and his followers fled to the safety of Canada. In 1881, his people starving, Sitting Bull surrendered and went onto a reservation. Upon his surrender Sitting Bull said, "I wish it to be remembered that I was the last man of my tribe to surrender my rifle."

For one year Sitting Bull performed in Buffalo Bill's Wild West Show. Always generous, he often gave his pay to poor white children. In 1890, because of fears that he was preparing to lead a Native American uprising, Sitting Bull was "accidentally" shot and killed while being arrested.

JOKES

Why did Buffalo Bill put a coat on his horse?
It was a little colt.

Why did Annie Oakley always carry a knife?
She was a sharpshooter.

Greenhorn: Buffalo Bill, what is the best way to mount a horse?
Buffalo Bill: I can't tell you, Sir. I'm not a taxidermist.

Annie: I'd like some lean buffalo meat for supper.
Waiter: Which way do you want it to lean, left or right?

What was Buffalo Bill's favorite sandwich?
A hero sandwich.

Sam: There's a man in the Wild West show who can jump on a horse's back, slip underneath, catch hold of its tail, and finish on its neck!
Dan: That's nothing. I did all of that the first time I rode a horse.

How did Annie Oakley make time go fast?
She used the spur of the moment.

What two things couldn't Annie Oakley eat for breakfast?
Lunch and dinner

Why did Annie Oakley eat bullets?
She wanted to grow bangs!

Why did Annie Oakley shoot in the oven?
She was a hot shot!

Annie: Bill, what is the best way to catch a fish?
Bill: Have someone throw one to you!

"Annie Oakley and the Wild West." *Cobblestone* Magazine. January, 1991.
Eisenberg, Lisa. *The Story of Sitting Bull: Great Sioux Chief.* Dell, 1991.
Stevenson, Augusta. *Buffalo Bill: Frontier Daredevil.* Simon and Schuster, 1991.

THE ALAMO

Dawn, March 6, 1836. A Mexican bugler sounds the attack. Two thousand Mexican soldiers shout, "Viva, Santa Anna!" as they charge the Alamo, an old Spanish mission. The 188 defenders inside the Alamo rally at their colonel's call, "Come on, boys! The Mexicans are upon us!"

Why were the Mexicans attacking the Texans? Texas was part of Mexico. To settle the wide open plains of Texas, the Mexicans invited Americans to settle there. However, over 30,000 poured into Texas. Soon these new Texans wanted their own government outside Mexican control. They wanted to make money from the rich cottonlands and to own slaves. Mexico wanted to keep Texas and to end slavery there. On March 2, 1836, the Texans declared their independence from Mexico.

General Santa Anna led his Mexican army against the rebelling Texans, surrounding many of them in the Alamo.

The Texans fought hard. But after twelve days of bombardment from Mexican cannons, the Alamo's walls were weakened and its defenders exhausted. Still, they turned back Santa Anna's first attack, then his second. But the third attack was too much. The Mexicans stormed the walls. The defenders fought on with guns, knives, tomahawks, pistols, even fists. One by one they fell. Colonel William Travis died from a gunshot wound. Davy Crockett, down from Tennessee to help his friends, died with seventeen dead Mexicans nearby. James Bowie, sick and in bed, shot two Mexican soldiers before dying himself.

From first bugle call to last bullet shot, the final battle of the Alamo lasted ninety minutes.

"Remember the Alamo!" became the cry of other Texans and Americans who wanted revenge on Santa Anna. Led by Sam Houston, these settler-soldiers met and defeated the Mexican army six weeks later. Santa Anna was captured and signed a paper giving Texas its independence.

On December 29, 1845, Texas became the twenty-eighth state of the United States.

JOKES

What did Sam Houston tell the cook when he ordered pie for dessert?
"Remember the a la mode!"

Why did Davy Crockett shoot a bull?
He wanted to hit a bull's-eye.

Tenderfoot: I'd like to buy a horse. How much are they?
Davy Crockett: Ten dollars apiece.
Tenderfoot: How much is a whole one?

There was a cook in the Alamo butcher shop. He was 6 feet tall and wore size 13 shoes. What did he weigh?
Meat!

Who was the worst shot at the Alamo?
Mr. Completely.

Who was the best shot at the Alamo?
Davy Crockett. He could make 100 frogs croak with one shot.

Jim: What three letters describe Santa Anna?
Davy: N M E.

What did one wall of the Alamo say to the other?
"I'll meet you at the corner."

Davy: Did you hear that Jim Bowie ate twenty-five pancakes?
Sam: How waffle!

How many big men were born on the Texas frontier?
None. Only babies are born in Texas!

"Remember the Alamo!" *Cobblestone* Magazine. March, 1982.
Fisher, Leonard Everett. *The Alamo.* Holiday House, 1987.
Stein, Conrad. *The Alamo.* Childrens Press, 1987.

OUTLAWS

Sheriff Pat Garrett looks at the paper in his hand. It is from the governor of New Mexico. "Therefore, you, the sheriff of the county, are commanded that on Friday, the 13th day of May, 1881, you take William Bonny, alias Kid, to some safe and convenient place and there hang the said Willam Bonny, alias Kid, by the neck until he is dead."

Sheriff Garrett picks up his pen to write back to the governor. How can he tell him that Billy the Kid has escaped?

However, two months later, Garrett does his duty. With one shot, he kills Billy the Kid. The Kid is only twenty-one years old.

There was little or no law west of the Mississippi for many years. Outlaws rustled cattle, robbed banks, stole horses. Many times the bandits were never caught. If they were, justice was swift. Horse thieves were hung. Cattle rustlers were run off or hung. Bank robbers were shot or put in jail.

Frank and Jesse James are two of the most famous outlaws. By age twenty Jesse James was the head of a band of gunslinging robbers. His brother Frank helped him in his robberies. With their gang, the James brothers held up banks, robbed trains, and killed anyone who dared get in their way. In 1881 a reward of $10,000 was offered for their capture, dead or alive. Jesse's time ran out when one of his gang members, eager for the reward, shot him in the back of the head as he was dusting a picture.

Lawmen slowly brought law and peace to the Wild West. Wild Bill Hickok, Wyatt Earp, the Texas Rangers, and U.S. marshals sought justice at the end of a gun barrel.

Why did Billy the Kid take guns to school?
The teacher said they were going to learn to draw!

Why didn't the outlaw take a bath?
He wanted to be filthy rich.

Why was the bandit cook so mean?
He would beat the eggs and whip the cream!

How strong were robbers?
They could hold up trains.

Billy the Kid spent months digging a tunnel out of jail. His tunnel ended up in a playground.
"I'm free!" he shouted.
The pioneer girl said, "So what! I'm four."

What did the boy's mother say when he turned red?
Wyatt, Burp!

What young goat robbed banks?
Billy the Kid.

Bank Teller: What has a head and a tail but no body?
Robber: A penny.

Why was the horse thief always in town?
He was hanging around!

Why did the outlaws rob the Missouri River?
It had two banks!

If a robber was in jail with only a bed and a calendar, how would he survive?
He would drink the water from the bed springs and eat the dates from the calendar.

Why was the bakery robbed so often?
Because the baker had so much dough.

Judge: Order in the court!
Outlaw: A hamburger with pickles for me.

Why wouldn't the bank robber take a bath?
He was a dirty crook!

Who was the only man the robber would take his hat off for?
The barber!

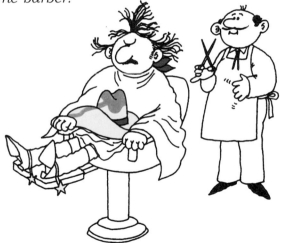

Herda, D. J. *Outlaws of the American West.* Millbrook Press, 1995.
Ross, Stewart. *Bandits and Outlaws.* Millbrook Press, 1995.
Savage, Jeff. *Gunfighters of the Wild West.* Enslow, 1995.

INDEX

ABOUT THE AUTHORS

Peter and Connie Roop are both teachers in the Appleton Area School District in Appleton, Wisconsin. Peter, who has a BA in Geology and an MA in Children's Literature, teaches science and social studies in grades 1 and 2. Connie, who also has a BA in Geology as well as an MA in Science Teaching, teaches environmental science in grades 11 and 12.

The Roops are avid travelers and spend their summers visiting scenic or historical sites, primarily for book research. When they're not on the road or in the air, the Roops live in Appleton with their children Sterling and Heidi.

ABOUT THE ARTIST

Anne Canevari Green is a freelance illustrator with a BA in Fine Arts from the College of New Rochelle. Formerly a book designer with a major publisher, she now works mainly in children's book illustration. Her most recent books include *Gifts to Make for Your Favorite Grownup* by Kathy Ross, *Surviving Homework: Tips from Teens* by Amy Nathan, and *Some Stuff*, a picture book by Elizabeth Ring.

The artist lives in Westhampton Beach, New York with her husband Monte who is a retired high school math teacher.